J
P
RABE

1/17
13.49

Super Rover's Space Adventure

By Tish Rabe
Based on a television script by Bob Ardiel
Illustrated by Tom Brannon

Random House 🏠 New York

Based in part on *The Cat in the Hat Knows a Lot About Space!* © CITH 3 Specials Inc. (a subsidiary of Portfolio Entertainment, Inc.), 2016.

THE CAT IN THE HAT KNOWS A LOT ABOUT THAT! logo and word mark TM 2010 Dr. Seuss Enterprises, L.P., Portfolio Entertainment, Inc., and Collingwood O'Hare Productions, Ltd. All rights reserved. The PBS KIDS logo is a registered trademark of PBS. Both are used with permission. All rights reserved.

Broadcast in Canada by Treehouse™. Treehouse™ is a trademark of the Corus® Entertainment Inc. group of companies. All rights reserved.

Visit us on the Web!   randomhousekids.com   Seussville.com   pbskids.org/catinthehat   treehousetv.com
Educators and librarians, for a variety of teaching tools, visit us at RHTeachersLibrarians.com
ISBN 978-0-399-55204-5   Library of Congress Control Number 2016935515
Printed in the United States of America
10 9 8 7 6 5 4 3 2 1
First Edition

"Nick and Sally," the Cat said,
"get ready to race
and meet Astronaut Audrey
way up in space.

"She has a surprise.
Hurry! Jump in!
Our space adventure
is about to begin!"

"Welcome!" said Audrey.
"Here's someone new—
Super Rover, my space dog,
is glad to meet you!

"He's on a mission to
show you the way
to see all eight planets—
in only one day."

They took off with a blast
and flew right past the sun.
"There's Mercury," said Nick,
"planet number one!
So close to the sun,
it's hot night and day."
"Look!" Sally said.
"Rover's flying away!"

They all flew to Venus
at zip-zapping speed.
"For space travel," said Nick,
"Rover's all that we need!"

"No one lives here," the Cat said,
"and we can see why.
Every day on Venus,
it is dusty and dry."

Next they flew past Earth,
third planet from the sun.
"People live on this planet," said Nick,
"but it's the only one."

"You're right!" said the Cat.
"It has water and air,
which are two reasons
we all can live there."

They flew even faster
and soared past the stars,
right to the fourth planet,
the Red Planet—Mars!

Then Sally noticed something
that seemed to be wrong.
Rover was missing—
the space dog was gone!

"There he is!" said Nick.
The dog shook all over.
"He's really in trouble.
We've got to help Rover!"

He was stuck in some space junk!
"Oh no!" Sally said.
"Rover's tangled in wires
from his paws to his head."

But the Cat in the Hat
knew just what to do:
"This is a job for
Thing One and Thing Two."

The Things got Rover untangled.
"Great job!" said the Cat.
Super Rover barked, "Thank you"
(or something like that!).

"Let's get going!" said Nick.
"We still need to explore.
We've been to four planets,
but there are four more."

When they got to Jupiter,
the Cat said, "See that spot?
Three Earths could fit in it,
believe it or not."

Next they swung past Saturn
and counted its rings.
"Space travel," said Sally,
"is like having wings!"

When they got to Uranus,
Nick said, "What a ride!"
"This planet looks tilted!"
the Cat then replied.

"Look! There's Neptune!" said Sally.
"Our mission is done.
It's the eighth planet,
farthest from the sun!"

"We'll be at the space station," the Cat said,
"in less than an hour."
Then suddenly they were caught in . . .
an asteroid shower!

Space rocks were falling
this way and that!
"Look out, Rover!" said Sally.
"Hold ON!" said the Cat.
"Push the Master-ma-blaster.
Let's get away quick!"
"An asteroid just crashed
into Rover!" cried Nick.

Rover began twirling and
swirling in space,
slipping and sliding
all over the place!

"He can't fly!" Sally said.
"Rover's going to crash."
But the Space-ama-racer
saved him in a flash!

"Thanks so much," Audrey said.
"I'm so proud of you.
You saved my space dog—
and saw eight planets, too!"

"He had some trouble," said Sally.
"But we got him fixed up.
Your Super Rover is truly
one special pup!"